Robert's Rules of Order

A Beginner's Guide to Robert's Rules of Order, Teaching You how to Manage and Run Meetings!

Table of Contents

Introduction

Thank you for taking the time to pick up this book all about Robert's Rules of Order!

This book covers the topic of Robert's Rules of Order, and will explain to you this powerful system for conducting meetings and making group decisions.

For over a century now, Robert's Rules have been used worldwide to assist in the conducting of meetings. The rules have been adopted by thousands of different business organizations, political groups, and even the United Nations.

The implementation of these rules will allow you to effectively run meetings, keep them fair, and allow for the best possible outcomes without unnecessarily wasting any precious time.

This book explains Robert's Rules in modern day English, and gives you a simple guide to follow for implementing these rules in your own business or organization.

 At the completion of this book you will have a good understanding of Robert's rules and possess the ability to implement them in your next meeting.

Once again, thanks for taking the time to read this book, I hope you find it to be helpful and informative!

Chapter 1:
What are Robert's Rules of Order?

Henry (Martyn) Robert was the creator of Robert's Rules of Order, and worked as an officer of engineering in the Army. When asked, suddenly, to lead a meeting at the local church, he realized he had no clue how to do this. He gave it his best shot, and was embarrassed by how it went, which inspired him to learn about parliamentary law. He then committed to never go to a meeting again until he mastered this. This led him to study and discover some reading on that topic, of which the selection was scarce.

Every so often, since he had duties in the military, he would travel to different parts of America, and found that everyone seemed to have different ideas of the right way to conduct meetings. No matter where he went, he couldn't' find a correct representation or formula for meetings. He was disappointed by this lack of order and consistency in the existing system, and thus decided that he would create his own rules. In order to give this chaos a bit of organization, he crafted Robert's Rules of Order, and we are still using them to this day. These rules have grown and shifted along with time, changing with the laws, but the essence remains the same, and the process remains helpful.

All Meetings can be Improved Upon with Robert's Rules:

I think all of us can relate to the feeling Robert had when he attended a meeting that seemed disastrous and accomplished little to nothing. Everyone has attended a meeting that appeared to have no structure or purpose at all. Meetings are foundational to a successful business, and improving them is a must for any company that wishes to remain relevant and efficient. These rules will help you learn how to head a meeting effectively, and will provide you the knowledge needed to keep every person engaged and active during the process.

Are these Rules Complicated or Hard to Understand?

Many people might cringe or groan when they hear these rules mentioned, due to a misconception that these rules are complicated. Meetings are already hard work without adding complex points to the equation. But even though the original book has some complex-sounding terms in it, the principles are easy.

- **Easy to Understand:** These principles can help anyone in need of some guidance or tips for running meetings, and are so easy to follow that even kids can benefit from them.

- **Versatility:** Although the author of these rules was likely not thinking of groups of kids when he wrote them, they encompass all meeting types. Even the United Nations use these rules.

- **They Work for Different Types and Sizes:** These rules work for all types and sizes of groups or meetings. Simply reading through the book can be a bit confusing, but that's what this guide is for.

A Brief Overview of the Rules:

We are going to delve into this topic in further detail in later chapters, but let's first explore a few key concepts that Robert's Rules of Order entail, to get you familiar with what it's all about.

- **Only Cover your own Work:** Those who work at a business have their own obligations to fulfill. You should allow committees to fulfill their commitments, and you should fulfill yours. Meetings are, in general, conducted in order to solve big problems. You will save a lot of time by allowing committees to handle any smaller issues that come up.

- **Don't Jump Around:** Multitasking has been proven to be inefficient time and time again, and business meetings are no exception. Conduct your orders of business separately, and do not jump around. Moving from item to item not only confuses everyone involved, but only slows down progress on every matter in the meeting.

- **Crosstalk is not Allowed:** Don't let crosstalk happen in your meetings, and instead instruct everyone speaking to refer to the head chairperson in the meeting. This will allow you to hold control over the meeting and let participants hear what they need to hear at the meeting.

- **Stay Focused:** The guidelines include keeping the discussion focused on whatever the topic is. This is important; so make sure that you tell speakers to stick to the topic, as well.

- **Know when to Cut a Topic off**: You should stop a discussion as soon as it starts being repetitive or redundant. For issues that are on the controversial side, decide upon a time limit ahead of time. As soon as the talk starts getting circular, sum up the talking points of each party and ask if there is anything to be added, or close the talk by announcing a motion (the definition of which will be covered shortly).

A well-run, ordered meeting works better for everyone involved, including the attendees and the officers. Following the guidelines listed above will help you to achieve this, but there is much more to know about Robert's Rules of Order. In the next chapter, we will review some key terms to make use of.

Chapter 2:
Key Terms to be Aware of

A meeting only works when it stays on task, allows everyone to be heard, and stays fair and focused. This will allow you to achieve more in less time, leading to increased satisfaction for all parties. When meetings are limited to a single hour, people are more likely to return the following month for another meeting. Following Robert's Rules of Order will help you keep your meetings short, sweet, and most importantly, productive.

Important Terms to Know for Robert's Rules:

When it comes to the procedures and terms of Robert's Rules, a few crucial fundamentals exist that everyone should know about. But first, let's start with some key terms to become familiar with.

- **A Motion:** This refers to a specific, formal method for proposing a matter that a vote is needed for. Whoever proposes this will say "I move that we…" and proceeds to clearly state the matter at hand that needs a vote. Another person at the meeting will then move to "second" this motion. The meeting's participants can then discuss this motion, with guidance from a president, until the time to vote comes.

- Then, the group's president will ask for a vote on those who are "in favor" then those who are "opposed". You might recognize these terms. Those who don't vote on the matter are known as abstentions, and will not be asked for since they don't get counted for the motion's final outcome. Members are not allowed to give their thoughts repeatedly for any motion.

- Some exceptions exist, however, if the current Speaker chooses not to follow that rule in certain circumstances. This is up to the Speaker's discretion and judgment according to the meeting and its subject matter. The members have to raise their hands to vote, and a list of the speaker is recorded to keep track of people who voted, along with their voting order.

- **A Motion's "Tabling":** At times, a motion may not be fit for voting, for whatever reason. This calls for the need to postpone, or table it, until another meeting can take place. Although, by the Rules, there would ideally be a newer motion to take its place, some groups can opt for another, simpler choice to just delay it. Some may find it helpful to decide upon a member or committee to research the problem and bring their findings to the following meeting. This technique is useful for saving time on a talk that may have gone circular, particularly when facts are missing.

- **The Agenda:** This includes a list of specified items, in detail, ordered in the fashion that they will be gone over. Put forth an order here, for business, that will be consistent in each and every meeting, and make sure every meeting attendee has a hard copy of this agenda. This agenda should be posted before the meeting. This should be specific about what the meeting will cover.

- **A Quorum:** This term refers to the minimum amount of attendees needed to follow through with the purpose of the meeting; business. Typically, this is a number decided by the bylaws of the group. If there is no specific quorum to be found, the Rules indicate that it should be set at a member majority.

- **The Minutes of a Meeting:** This refers to the record, in a permanent sense, of whatever business happened at the meeting, which is usually arranged by the secretary of the group. The minutes will include information such as the location, time, and date that the meeting took place, along with the quorum, and the officer who presided over the meeting in question. In this record, motions, along with the outcomes of those motions (excluding specified counts of votes) are included, as well.

- The minutes, however, do not typically record conversation. At each meeting, the minutes are put before the attendees for approval, when the time for the next meeting arrives. This method can be useful for your business meetings at work, and you will find out exactly how so in chapter seven of this guide.

- **Adjournment:** This is a simple concept that refers to a formal closing of a group meeting, allowing everyone to know that the session is over. This detail will be documented in the minutes of that meeting for possible later reference.

- **Amendments:** Motions are able to be changed by motions that follow. If both the initial mover and the person who seconded the motion agree to this amendment, this is considered a friendly amendment and doesn't need another seconder. This agreement is also not up for debate. If, however, this amendment is not considered or named friendly, a seconder is needed. This motion then must get debated and then voted on.

Points in Robert's Rules of Order:

Points are specific motions that are more important than other motions or talking topics. They are so serious that they allow speakers to be interrupted and do not need someone to second them.

- **Points of Order:** These may be raised if an individual thinks that the business of a meeting is not proceeding in the correct fashion. Then, a speaker needs to either disagree or agree with the raised point. This may also be used if an individual doesn't understand what's going on in the meeting or proceedings, or if they need more details on something specific.

- **Points of Privilege:** These may be raised if an individual feels as though they have had their rights, as a member, violated in some way. This may also be appropriate if someone can't participate at the meeting because of trouble hearing the person speaking, uncomfortable temperature conditions in the room, or because they are unclear about procedure details. If, for some reason, you are unclear about what is going on in the meeting, you may interrupt the person speaking and ask for more details using this point.

- **Points of Information**: This is one of the least understood points in Robert's Rules of Order, and should be used in order to request information that you think is needed in order for you to understand a debate. This point is not intended to be used for giving out information. A member can choose to give no answer to this query by not giving up the floor at that time. It's worth reiterating that despite its name, this is not intended to give out information.

- **Points of Challenge to a Speaker:** This is intended to be used when someone is not in agreement with the ruling a Speaker has just made. The person disagreeing has to state exactly why they disagree, which then allows the Speaker to explain why they made their ruling. Then a vote follows to see where everyone stands on that ruling.

Chapter 3:
When should these Rules be Used?

When getting acquainted with Robert's Rules of Order, you need first to figure out when and why your meeting must take place. After this is established, you should invite a small number of people, ideally making the group 12 members or less. These rules should be used in the following instances:

- **When you have a Specific Purpose:** These rules should be used at meetings where a specific purpose is in mind, and once this is established, do everything within your power to stick to that purpose. In order to do this, holding smaller meetings is best, because it's easier to keep all members on a similar wavelength. This makes it more likely that your meeting members will have the same goal in mind and that clarifications can be made if necessary.

- **When they can be Informal:** Your meetings should be small and mostly informal, gathered with the intention of allowing everyone to give their opinion and participate. You should sit in such a way that everyone can see each other and look each other in the eye, working your way around this circle and letting everyone take their turn to talk. Some of your participants will decline to speak when it's their first turn, but may later on hear something said that reminds them of a thought they want to share, and will do so on the next turn.

- The circle is of utmost importance, since without this form, you might have people trying to take over the flow of conversation, or people on the opposite end of the spectrum, reluctant to share their ideas. The circle format gives everyone a fair chance to share their ideas, without too much pressure.

- **When Debate needs to Flow:** When you don't purposely limit the debate that happens in the meeting, you get a more genuine idea exchange, with honest opinions and ideas. Although this might sound difficult, when you work with smaller groups, a common purpose will typically keep things in order. The Speakers of the group should know that there is always another person waiting to speak.

- **When you need Solutions:** In most meetings, single members taking over can be an issue, and the rules give a concrete solution to this problem. The great part about these rules is that you can tweak them to fit your own needs, even adding your own rules. One recommended idea for this is imposing a limit on how long each participant can speak, for just a few minutes, for example. However, they must be allowed their turn again the next time around.

- **To Help with Focus:** You can also make a cellphone or tablet ban for the meeting, since this can distract from having everyone's focus on the issue at hand. This problem of distraction means that the members can leave having entirely opposite ideas of what happened there. Some meeting leaders choose to appoint a note-taker, and then have them send the minutes around to everyone after the meeting, to see that all members agree about the meeting events.

- No one enjoys listening to someone drone endlessly, which happens too often at meetings. Far too often, this is the leader of the meeting, and although this person is meant to guide the meeting, they're not intended to do all of the work. In fact, contrary to what some may think, the leader of the meeting shouldn't always be at the center of all the action.

- **When Everyone needs a Fair Shot to Speak:** People leading meetings often take over the entire talk. How it usually goes is a participant gives their opinion, then the leader answers, then someone else speaks, and the leader answers, another person talks, and again the leader responds. This format is what causes so many to be bored by meetings. A better structure is allowing everyone at the meeting to talk before the chair answers anyone. In order to make this format even more productive, the leaders should talk to the participants before meetings to ask them what they want to contribute and what they are expecting.

- This can give the leader inspiration for what to cover in the meeting, choosing what they and the staff agree are crucial talking points. Robert's Rules of Order encourage thinking on a critical scale before the meeting even takes place.

Although some may believe that Robert's Rules are complex or out of date, one only needs to sit through a poorly managed meeting to see value in them. This is age old wisdom that will always be useful in any business setting that requires conversation.

Chapter 4:
How to Use Robert's Rules of Order

In order to use Robert's Rules of Order, one only needs to absorb what they truly represent, and start applying them at work. Here are some ideas for using them at your place of business or wherever else they may be needed:

- **Hand Out a Copy of Robert's Rules:** Depending on your business, it may be appropriate and useful to print out a copy of Robert's Rules for your office to review. This is recommended if your place of business deals with law or is more on the formal side.

- **Hand Out the Rules in your Own Words:** For others, handing out a copy of the Rules, written in your own words, may be a better idea. You could also write out excerpts from this book to give to your employees, students, or anyone else you think could benefit from a summary of Robert's Rules. Next, we'll cover some simplified points from Robert's Rules that can improve how smoothly your meetings go, starting now.

Robert's Rules, Simplified:

- All are allowed their chance to speak.

- Everyone should know what is happening in the meeting.

- The Speaker may only be interrupted if it's extremely important.

- Only one matter is discussed at a time.

How to Use Robert's Rules of Order:

- **When you wish to Present an Idea:** To do this, you must first be recognized by the group's president, then proceed to present your idea (motion). In order for this to be considered or debated, you must receive a second for your motion.

- **You wish to Cancel a Motion:** If you wish to cancel a motion that someone else introduced, you need to say that you object for that motion to be considered. You don't have to receive recognition to do this, but it has to happen before debate arises. To do this, you don't need to receive a second, and this is not up for debate, only requiring a vote of 2/3.

- **You wish to Change Words of a Motion:** When you wish to change the wording of a motion being debated, first receive the president's recognition. You can then move on to adding new words, striking some, or both adding and striking certain words.

- **You want to Move on from a Debate at Present:** You can opt for limiting a current debate, or by only designating a specified number of people to speak. This needs at least a vote of 2/3 to pass.

- **You are done Listening to the Debate:** You may opt for closing a current debate, which requires a vote of at least 2/3. You can also move on to the question that occurred previously, which will cut the debate off where it is and allow the meeting members to vote.

- **You wish to Postpone:** For postponing motions, call for tabling the motion in question. This can happen after at least one business item has occurred. A motion is considered dead if it has not been taken off the "table" when the following meeting comes to an end. In order to cancel or kill a specific motion when it becomes tabled, you need a vote of at least 2/3.

- **You need a Break:** This is simple and only consists of asking to move to a recess period for a specific amount of time. To end a meeting, simply ask if the meeting can be adjourned.

- **Your Mind has been Changed on a Vote:** If you wish to shift your perspective on a matter that was already voted on during that meeting, which you voted for, and also won, request a reconsideration. This will be put up for a majority vote, allowing that motion to return to the floor and cancelling the previous vote.

Interruption of the Speaker:

This is typically not allowed or okay in meetings based around Robert's Rules of Order, but there are a few exceptions. You can only interrupt the meeting's speaker when:

- **You need Clarification on Business Information:** If you are unclear about some of the details surrounding a business item of the meeting, you may interrupt the Speaker at a meeting.

- **You need Clarification about Rules:** If, for some reason, you are unclear on rules at the meeting, you may interrupt to make a parliamentary inquiry.

- **Privilege Reasons:** This includes not being able to hear the person speaking, being unsafe, or uncomfortable, and is called a question of privilege, according to Robert's Rules of Order.

- **You see Rules being Broken:** You are allowed to interrupt if you see rules being broken in the meeting, which is referred to as a point of order.

- **Disagreement:** You are allowed to interrupt the speaker if you find yourself disagreeing with a ruling the president has passed, and need only to request an appeal.

Influence over Discussion at Meetings:

Another benefit to Robert's Rules is that you have a say in everything that occurs in business meetings. You can influence discussion at meetings if:

- **You want to Discuss a Matter:** This is called a motion.

- **You wish to Change a Matter:** This is referred to as an amendment.

- **You want to Limit the Debate Happening:** This is simply called "limit debate".

- **You wish for Evaluation and a Report:** This is called "commit".

Chapter 5:
The Benefits of Using Robert's Rules

This chapter will cover some of the advantages of getting familiar with Robert's Rules. The language that Robert's Rules were written in is considered quite formal, and since this is a modern, beginner's guide, understandable terminology will be used. Although Robert's Rules of Order were written and based upon procedures of a parliamentary nature, they are designed to work for any and all meetings, no matter the business or organization. The book of Robert's Rules is timeless, and on its eleventh edition at the moment. It has been and remains a great point of reference for people who wish to improve the way they run their meetings. Here are some benefits that are available to you when you use these rules.

You are able to Learn, Adopt, and Experiment with Them:

Although the rules are, of course, rules, they are actually quite flexible. The first step here is to begin and figure out how these rules will work for you. Ideally, they will of course make your meetings fairer, more orderly, faster, and all around better. You can then grow your implementation and knowledge of the rules further, incorporating them into your meeting structure.

You can Postpone Discussion Topics:

Robert's Rules allow you some measure of control over what happens in the meetings you attend. In fact, you can indefinitely postpone a motion, deciding that the motion in question shouldn't be talked about more at that meeting. This, however, doesn't rule out that topic being brought up at a future meeting, later on. This suggestion must be voted upon and also seconded to go into effect.

You can End Debates in your Meetings with Robert's Rules:

You can call to motion a "question", which allows you to end a debate, and get to a vote for a motion. This must be seconded by someone else, similar to how other actions work. Once a vote has been taken and the majority has decided, it can pass.

Using the Rules, you can Change Existing Motions:

This is done using amendments. There are times when a motion must change, even after debate on it has already occurred. If someone suggests this, a vote must be taken, along with a second to go into effect. When this idea has been accepted, it can stay.

You can Request Further Research:

Sometimes, getting objectively factual information can be hard, and being well-informed is a must for any good business. With Robert's Rules, you can request that motions be researched on more, by another committee. Then, a report will be given to you at the following meeting with that committee's findings. This can be assigned to a committee that already exists, or one that was just organized, but needs to be voted on and seconded in order to pass.

You can Ensure that Discussion runs Smoothly:

We all know how unpredictable meetings can be, and Robert's Rules of Order allow them to go smoothly. You won't ever have to again wonder whether this upcoming meeting will accomplish anything or not. Here are some guidelines for making sure this happens:

- **Use Hand Raising:** When you want to talk, raise your hand, and wait for your turn to give your opinion.

- **Give your Department and Name:** This should occur before you begin talking about the issue.

- **Stay on Topic:** Try to only talk about the motion or topic that is currently in question. If you want to talk about something else, implement the new business or question period options.

- **Don't Repeat:** Whenever possible, don't repeat the points that others have made already. The exception to this rule is when you have a new idea to add to the current point.

Chapter 6:
How to Implement these Rules in your Workplace

If you've already decided that the rules can help you in your workplace, all you need to do is become familiar with them. The fact that they have been used for over a century proves their effectiveness. In order to use them, here are some steps you can begin taking to use them in your work's conference calls or meetings:

Get to Know the Intent and Spirit of them:

It isn't always the most practical choice to use Robert's Rules of Order word by word, in their original format. Since you are operating in a modern day business, from a modern day understanding, you will likely need to shift the rules and adapt them to fit your needed situation. You may have a variety of locations, situations, purposes, and types of meetings to handle, all of which must be covered.

You will find it helpful to get to know the rules intimately, getting familiar with their design and purpose, overall. The rules are meant to give an orderly and fair structure by which to direct meetings, from which will lead to outcomes that are democratic. They should be constructive; helping rather than hindering progress in your business and each member of the meeting. Here are some guidelines you should study and memorize in order to make the most of the rules:

- **Maintaining Order and Control:** The host or chair of your meeting has to keep control over the meeting, in order to ensure that it is conducted in the most orderly and fair way possible.

- **Attention and Focus in the Meeting:** You should stay focused on the meeting's subject, refraining from going off topic yourself, and steering members back to the subject at hand, when necessary.

- **Fairness:** You must allow every participant to have their turn to talk, before you let another meeting member talk twice. Meeting members should talk to the host when giving their remarks and stay professional at all times. Even in businesses where everyone is friends, a formal and professional setting is conducive to productive and efficient meetings.

- **Politeness:** Courteousness and politeness is of crucial importance, according to the rules. This should take care of most ulterior motive issues or clashes in personality of meeting members.

Sometimes, members at your meeting will have strong opinions on a matter being discussed. Each of these members has every right to give their opinion, as long as it is presented persuasively and respectfully. Incorporating and understanding some of the rules and guidelines here will aid members in presenting input that is meaningful and relevant, also aiding business calls and meetings in staying on task.

Adapting Robert's Rules to your Unique Business:

As soon as you have a fair understanding of the general guidelines for making use of the rules, you can pick and choose the rules that are relevant to our business, adapting them to make sense to you. There are a few useful rules to start with, and not all of them must be used or adapted. Choose only the rules that are relevant to your business, and yourself, and use the ones that will help you with your meetings. To begin with, you can start simply using the following guidelines in your meetings or conference calls:

- **Tabling:** When you need to suspend any further talk on a specific matter, you can use this, but refrain from interruption, when possible. This lets you move to another issue or item on the agenda. This is not up for debate, and requires a second and a majority vote. This is most useful when a conversation appears to be trailing off into irrelevant directions, but keeps it polite.

- **Group Dynamic**: When the situation arises that requires a group of people, the first order of business is agreement about what they are doing, along with the particulars on how it will be done. As stated earlier, 12 people or less is ideal, but you can have up to 15 and it can still work. When it goes above 15, a formal arrangement with tighter control will help you stay on task, without compromising the fairness of the meeting or arrangement.

- **The Chair**: One person must be assigned as the chair of the meeting, with the responsibility of keeping things orderly. Although being fair in every single situation is impossible even for the best of people, they should be able to do this at least the majority of the time.

Beginning, Running, and Ending your Meetings:

- **Your Meeting's Chairman:** There must be one person who acts as the presider over your meetings, called, as stated above, the chair, or chairman. They are only referred to as this if they have been specifically elected to run that meeting.

- **Your Meeting's President:** However, if this person is elected to serve for at least a year, they will earn the title "president", but still be called the chair of the meeting while they are presiding over it.

- **Shared Ideas and Responsibility:** One main focus of Robert's Rules of Order is sharing ideas and responsibility in meetings and business, in general. No organization should be subject to following orders or ideas from a small group of people. This is why the quorum, discussed earlier (the minimum amount of people present at a meeting) is put into effect. This number is decided upon by the organization itself, and it's typically over half of the organization's members.

- **Invalid Actions for Robert's Rules:** That being said, if any actions are taken that are substantive, they are invalid if the quorum is not present for that meeting. This protects fairness for the organization.

- **Beginning a Meeting Officially:** The meeting officially starts when the presiding officer officially announces so by saying that "the meeting is coming to order". However, in less formal settings, this doesn't need to be explicitly stated that way. The chair of the meeting should then announce that the minutes will be read by the secretary, asking if any corrections must be made to them. The minutes can then be approved after any needed changes are made to them.

- Sometimes, drafts of the minutes are sent out from the meeting before, by the secretary, before the meeting which they must be approved at can begin. The participants of the meeting then must hear any necessary reports from the committees, boards, or officers of the business or organization. This may be a general request, or a specific member's report that is needed. If there are actions which have been recommended, they should be in the report, to be voted and debated on after the report.

- **Unfinished Items from the Last Meeting:** If there is any unfinished business from the last meeting, it can be now be brought up, to be voted and debated on, in hopes of reaching a conclusion or decision. This will include actions or items which were being discussed at the previous meeting, or being decided upon, in addition to items that should have been covered at the previous meeting but were not brought up or discussed due to adjournment.

- **Old and New Business in Robert's Rules:** Old business does not exist in the rules, and you shouldn't ever try to revisit matters that already have been settled in a previous meeting. The chair of the meeting may ask if new business exists, which then sets the stage for members to start a related motion to their business. Rather than going with a standard business order, meetings or groups can opt for an agenda, instead. This will give a specified order to consider each item, and at times, will give specific time allotments for them to be discussed or debated upon.

- The agenda has to become adopted by a vote of majority or very soon after the meeting begins. Prior to the agenda being adopted, changes must be made to it. As mentioned earlier, adjourning refers to closing a meeting. Once the meeting has reached its end, it's up to the chair to ask if anyone has further business to bring up. When there is none, the meeting can be officially closed, or adjourned.

- **Adjourning with Unfinished Business:** A meeting may be adjourned, even when there is still business to settle, but only been the majority votes for this to occur.

- **Pauses and Breaks in the Meeting:** Whenever the meeting members wish to take a pause or break in the meeting, they can vote to have a short recess period, which will last around five minutes or so, typically. The meeting's chair can pause the meeting, if no one objects to this, by asking for group members to take a break, called "standing at ease". What this refers to is the group members remaining seated, talking amongst themselves, in some cases, until the meeting is again called to order.

Using Motions in your Meeting:

When a decision must be made, the process is begun by the proposal of beginning a motion, which is a member's formal proposal of specific action being taken by the group. The main motion has an introduction that brings up business matters in front of the group as a whole, and must be handled only one at a time, in succession.

- **Making Motions in the Meeting:** In order to speak during a debate or start a motion while a meeting is happening, you must stand right after the current speaker finishes, letting the chair know that you want to say something. If the chair says you can, you are recognized officially as the speaker, and you can now start talking. This means that the floor is yours for the time being.

- **Closing your Motion:** As soon as you're done, make sure you sit down to let others know that you are yielding the floor and another person can take over it. This allows everyone to know that you are finished for now.

- **Motion Amendments in your Meeting:** You can request or propose the idea of amending motions, and when this happens, the meaning and wording of the motion can both be changed. These requests for amendments must first have a second, which will lead them to be debated on prior to the vote. These amendments must specify where changes to the motion should be made, with specific words that will be used for this.

- When this amendment is voted on, it is only to decide whether details of the motion will change or not, and doesn't put the motion into effect or decide if it will get adopted or not. After any amendments are made, a vote will be collected for that motion, with its changes in place. Although the easiest amendments to make are the ones that add or insert certain words, they may also remove them, or both insert and remove words from the motion. This can help with making the document easily understandable as well. If you are dealing with a long motion, adding or removing paragraphs can help organize it into a more readable format.

- **Amendment Voting in your Meeting:** For taking votes on amendments, the amendment should be stated by the meeting's chair, reading the motion as though it had already been changed. They should then clearly state that this was the amendment, and that the following vote will cover changes to the motion, not decide whether or not the motion will be passed in the end. When the results of the amendment vote have been cast and counted, it's up to the chair to re-read the motion as it now is, with or without changes.

- As soon as the full group, including all of its members, has cast their votes for a certain amendment, this settles the matter entirely, and it is not up for debate anymore. You may not, for example, suggest an additional amendment to put similar words into the motion, if the entire group voted out the insertion of specific words. This would be considered a misuse of the amendment.

Using Debate in your Meeting, According to Robert's Rules:

- **Debate Time:** You can talk up to two times on a motion being debated, in one day. You are allowed to talk for 10 minutes or less, although businesses can come up with their own rules for this, if they wish to do so. You are not allowed to transfer or save this time you are given.

- **Speaking Time:** The meeting's chair must recognize the next speaker, who should fairly be the person who first rises after the current one is done, and has already taken their seat again. Do not attempt to signal your wish to talk next, if someone still has the floor.

- **Speaking Preferences:** When you have made a motion, this gives you preference in discussing that motion, but only for one time. Usually, whoever makes a motion will be the first person to talk about it. Although it's true that all members can talk up to twice on one motion in one day, if someone hasn't talked yet, they automatically have preference over those who have had their turns to speak about the motion.

- As soon as the chair of the meeting is aware that people who both wish to have the floor have opposing ideas about the motion, they should attempt to fairly alternate between both, giving them equal speaking time.

- **Staying on Topic:** During debate of a particular motion, you have to speak only about the motion being discussed. This will, at times, have an effect on whether that motion becomes adopted or not, so tread carefully here.

- **Keeping it Objective, not Personal:** This may go without saying, but during a debate of a motion, only discuss the issue at hand, and not the person speaking. It is the issue at hand, and not the meeting member, that should be debated on. You can help to prevent personal debates by phrasing your ideas as though you're addressing the chair, instead of the other group members present. You should do this, even when you have a question that involves another member of the meeting.

- **Using Names during a Debate:** You shouldn't even use names of group members while a debate is in progress, as this is considered personal and unprofessional. Again, you should always keep the discussion about the issue being debated, not members.

- **Extend or Limit:** You may extend or limit the debate, or at least attempt to by introducing a motion. This can be done by limiting a current motion to a set period of time, like an hour, or suggesting a specific time of day that the debate or meeting will come to an end, when people can vote on the matter at hand. You may both give speeches of more or less time, or allow group members to talk more than twice, in some cases.

- **Ending a Debate:** When you wish to bring an end to a current debate, completely, a special motion must be introduced. This is called a previous question motion, or a close debate motion. When this motion has been adopted, the debate is instantly closed, and cannot be postponed for later, committed, or amended. When this motion is adopted, additional motions cannot be made, the exception being motions that were stated but not yet voted on beforehand.

- When this motion is introduced and wins by a majority vote of at least 2/3 of members, it may not be debated on, and is quite final. In order to close the debate right away, a group member needs to take the floor and call for a vote, immediately, on whatever question is being debated. This can then go into effect once someone seconds the motion and the majority votes for it. This ends the debate.

Committees and Postponing in Robert's Rules:

You can try to postpone a meeting or discussion to a later date, allowing the motion to be paused for the time being. You may also attempt to add an amendment to the postponing motion, which would, for example, state that a decision should be made at the next meeting, instead of at this one.

- **Decision Postponement:** If you wish to put a decision off until later, request to postpone it to a specified time, second this, and get a majority vote on the matter that agrees with this time frame. Usually, you can't do this for meetings that go beyond the upcoming meeting, or more than three months later than the current meeting.

- **Redraft and Additional Study:** Sometimes, it's helpful to study further or redraft the current motion, with a small number of members. It might, for example, require too much time to change the motion, or it may be the case that you need more information. If this is the case, handing it over to a specified committee for additional changes or study can help the group reach a more informed decision.

- This is known as "commit", and refers to a motion that hands the motion over to a committee. For this to happen, the majority must vote for it to be so, and a specific list of the individuals taking this over must be mentioned and explicitly made known. This may also include specific instructions for that committee, such as the date that it must be returned by.

- **Special vs. Standing Groups:** There are a couple of different committees, one of which is called a standing committee. These have a function and existence that continues on beyond one motion or meeting, and typically specialize in a specific subject or act. A special committee, on the other hand, is called together to accomplish one specific task, and is no longer in existence after the task has been accomplished.

- **Amendments for Committees:** It is possible to amend the choice of committing, both for changing a special committee's makeup, or changing some instructions. This can also be brought up for debate, but this should not be over the wish to refer the motion to commit, or any details covering a referral.

- **Group Committee Members:** The act of selecting the members and chairperson of committees is different throughout different groups. Usually, they are decided upon by the group president, when they first take their office term. Either that, or they get elected by the meeting members during the meeting that elects the officers of the group. Typically, they will serve a period that lasts the same amount of time as the group officers.

How to go about Mistake Correction using Robert's Rules:

As soon as a motion is brought up and settled during a meeting, an additional motion that covers that exact question must not be raised again during that meeting.

- **Changing is Harder than Instating:** In order to keep decisions as stable as possible, it's harder to change an action that was previously decider upon, than to make an action. Reconsideration may happen when a motion is first chosen, then one person who was in the winning side of the vote wishes to reconsider it. This must happen in the same meeting, however. This motion may only be taken on the exact day of the vote, the exception being a group meeting over a course of more than one day, which allows for voting to take place the following day.

- Remember that a reconsideration motion has no effect on the original choice, but if the reconsideration gets approved, the original choice or issue comes back into debate, and must be voted on.

- **Reconsidering or Rescinding a Motion:** If a meeting has ended and you can no longer reconsider that particular motion, you can request to amend a motion that was adopted previously, or request to rescind it. You are allowed to make both motions referred to previously, whether you voted for or against the original one, in addition to other times once the motion has been decided on already.

- For this to happen, you need notice to be previously made of your intention to put forth one of the motions. This will allow members to know what is happening, and to give them a chance to make it to that meeting. Both types of motions are considered main motions. You must treat it this way unless directed to do otherwise with notice ahead of time, backed up by a majority vote.

- **Renewing a Motion:** You may attempt to make a motion once it has been defeated already, at another meeting, and this is referred to as renewal. For this to happen, you must attempt to make that motion when you next have a meeting, regardless of the way you originally voted for it. This allows you to make up for mistakenly making a vote the first time, or lets you change your mind when needed.

Using Voting in your Meetings:

We have already briefly discussed the way voting works, according to Robert's Rules of Order, but this is worth going into more detail about, and there are some more points to be aware of.

- **Majority Votes:** This is usually required in order to elect someone to office or to adopt a proposed motion at a meeting. As mentioned before, this has to be over half of the group's members, and at times, 2/3 of the group members. This does not account for absent members, and you only need a majority of the present members in order to pass a motion.

- A majority vote of your whole group is needed when you are trying to amend a motion that was adopted previously, or rescind. A majority vote of the whole membership means the complete amount of people who count as the body of voters, during the time that the vote takes place, regardless of whether or not they are there.

- **When are 2/3 Votes Needed?** There are times when you need at least 2/3 to vote for a motion to pass, including trying to extend debate limits, close a debate, limit it, or suspend your organization's rules for some current matter. A vote of 2/3 is considered as such when the votes are cast by qualified members, not counting abstentions or blanks. This only applies when your meeting has its quorum present at the time.

- **Consent Unanimously in the Group:** If it appears that a motion has no opposition at all, a vote is not needed, under the principle of unanimous consent. This concept allows an action to happen or a motion to go into effect, without needing a vote or a debate to happen. When this occurs, the group's chair will ask members if anyone objects to that action being taken, and if no one does, will announce that the action is agreed upon and passed.

- **Voting Rights and Fairness:** All members can vote, with the exception of their rights to vote being suspended from a process of formal discipline. The chair of the group, or the officer presiding at that time, needs to stay impartial, allowing both sides of the matter, and all members involved, to feel as though they have been treated fairly. It is not allowed for the chair to be involved in a debate, as far as participating, unless they volunteer to give up their chair for that time.

- **Is the Chair allowed to Vote**?: The group's chair is only allowed to vote when their vote would have a deciding effect on the results, or when that vote is conducted by ballot. This means that for a vote that ties, a chair can vote in order to sway the results. They may also choose to tie it, if only one vote is needed and they wish to cast theirs. This applies, as well, when a motion is needing a vote of at least 2/3.

- **How does the Group Cast their Votes**? Group members are allowed to vote by using their voice, raising their hand, standing, or casting a ballot. This is up to the discretion of the chair or the group president at the time, and may vary depending on the matter at hand. A ballot is typically used where secrecy for results are required. Whoever collects and distributes the ballots for a vote must make sure that it's a fair vote, with each member voting only one time. They will then count the results and compose a report on their findings.

Elections and Nominations for your Meetings:

Nominations are proposals, announced formally to group members, and suggesting a certain individual to take a position or office for an upcoming election. Typically, these nominations occur, followed by a narrowing of voting to willing and qualified members or candidates for the position.

- **How to do this:** When a candidate is nominated from the floor, it's quite a simply process, and the chair asks for nominations referring to a specific position. Members who want to nominate a certain person should announce that person's name, and the process ends once all have nominated, who had a wish to do so.

- **Using a Committee for Nominations:** You may also choose candidates by nominating with a committee. These members must not be appointed, but elected instead. This committee must choose a single candidate for different officers, getting the consent of the nominee before doing this. This committee should then report, during the same meeting which the election takes place (or the one before that), which will then allow the members to officially be nominated.

- **How do these Elections take place?** Typically, these elections are done using a ballot. When just a single candidate for the office in question is nominated, the group's chair can officially announce that that nominee has been elected. Alternatively, a vote done by ballot can happen. For the situation where no one candidate gets the majority vote, another ballot will be cast, and another, until there is a decision based on majority vote.

- The ballot will retain every candidate, with the exception of voluntarily withdrawn candidates. The election is considered final when a candidate has accepted their position, and when the results become officially given and announced to all members of the group. Although some exceptions exist, when specified so, the candidate will accept their office immediately after their election has been finalized.

When Special Changes or Rules are Needed:

Although guidelines like Robert's Rules of Order are helpful, ultimately, every business and every group is different. Regulating specific business conduct, during meetings, should happen by the group's specified rules. These are typically alike throughout different groups, and Robert's Rules of Order are one prime example.

- **Unique Circumstances:** When the group discovered that a change to rules is needed from how they are in the book, they can choose to instate unique rules that supersede rules that conflict in that rule book. These changes must be voted on by a 2/3 vote in order to be adopted and officially pass and go into effect.

- **The Suspension or Enforcement of Group Rules:** Although the chair typically oversees the conduct of business at group meetings, it is the group itself, instead of the group's chair that holds the ultimate authority of rule violations. When you are in disagreement with something that the chair has ruled, you are able to appeal this to the entire group and all its members.

- To appeal, you must have a second. This can also become a matter of debate with the members of the group, and each group member is only allowed to talk one time. This will be followed by a vote that decides whether or not the decision will be appealed officially. A time may come when you wish to break a rule in the group's book, depending on the specific situation and all its considerations. If this situation arises, you are allowed to suggest suspending the existing rules. This must be followed by a second, and a majority vote of at least 2/3 to go into effect.

Chapter 7:
Using Minutes in your Meetings

Minutes are crucial to the success of meetings, since they are the single record that has survived to denote what happened or was said in meetings. These notes can be quite boring or dry, but it's a good thing if this is the case. The important thing is that these notes are simple to navigate and informative, giving the reader all they need to be aware of, even years after the original meeting took place.

When will Minutes come in Handy?

Any time you contact someone, such as a parliamentarian, to seek help, they will likely request to review the relevant minutes. They may also need access to an important piece of that information, such as specific words given in an amendment, or voting information that is relevant to the matter at hand.

- **Simplicity of Review and Use:** This simple and easy organization of meeting information and employment of language that is unpretentious, are qualities you should ensure that your minutes have.

- **Your Minutes should have Readability:** The minutes should be easy to read, as stated above, but it's important that they are also precise and informative. They should denote actions that were taken, giving facts in a clearly memorialized way.

How to Compose Minutes for your Meeting:

This might sound confusing at first glance, but luckily, Robert's Rules of Order give you precisely what you need to put on the minutes.

- **Your First Paragraph:** To be included in this paragraph is the type of meeting that was held (annual, special, or regular meeting). You should also include the organization or business name, along with the location, time, and date of that meeting (but don't write down location if it hasn't changed or always occurs at the same place). You also need a statement that confirms your secretary and regular officer who preside are there at the meeting.

- If they are not present, give the specific names of the substitutes. In the first paragraph, you should also mention if the minutes of the meeting before were approved and read, along with the date that the previous meeting took place. When corrections to minutes are made, they must be recorded in those minutes.

- **The Body of the Minutes:** Your body should include every main motion that was taken (with the exception of withdrawn minutes), and the specific name of whoever made the mentioned motion. You do not, however, need to include the name of the person who seconded in the minutes. You should also include the motions that bring questions up before the meeting attendees (but not withdrawn ones). Put, as well, the wording that was finally used in the motions, and whether they were disposed of or decided upon.

- Include vote information, along with the numbers of each vote, the ballot vote, and roll call vote. You should also put, in the body, secondary motions which were not withdrawn or lost, along with any existing notices about motions, appeals, points of order, dispositions, and any related reasons for these. Include full text on whatever the meeting assembly has requested to be included in your minutes, although this doesn't occur often.

- **The Final Paragraph:** In this section, put the hour that the meeting was adjourned. Nothing else needs to be included, but there are some other considerations to keep in mind in regards to finalizing the minutes. The entire committee's proceedings don't need to be put into your minutes, but you should include reports or any moves into committee into the minutes. When questions are, for some reason, informally considered, you should record it in the same way as you would with typical rules.

- Being informal in meetings is only allowed when additional chances to debate are put on the table or otherwise allowed. The entire text of reports should be put into the minutes, but only when this is ordered by the assembly or members of the meeting in question. You should write down guest speaker names, if there are any, along with presentation subjects, but don't make summaries about the remarks of the Speaker.

Guidelines for How to Sign your Minutes:

You should only have your minutes signed by your secretary, and sometimes, your president. Since the minutes are the legal recording of the proceedings of your meetings, the signature of your secretary gives credibility to the authenticity of this document.

- **Approval of your Minutes:** Your meeting's minutes need to be approved when the next meeting occurs, after the opening routines and calls to order. When the meeting becomes adjourned, you should approve your previous meeting's minutes before you take up any remaining business that was left at the previous meeting. In addition, the adjourned meeting's minutes must get approved when the next regular or adjourned meeting occurs.

- **Unofficial Minutes:** When minutes have been drafted before a meeting, they don't count as official unless and until they have been approved by group members. Since it's possible for changes to the minutes to be made, before approval, the group's secretary should take note somewhere that this is a draft that needs approval. Once these minutes have been approved, the group's secretary should include corrections or changes in the minute's margin. In addition, she or he should retype those minutes to cover what was corrected. After this, they should write that the minutes were approved and initial the record, along with the date.

Conclusion

Thanks again for taking the time to read this book!

You should now have a good understanding of Robert's Rules of Order, and how they can be used to effectively conduct a meeting!

If you enjoyed this book, please take the time to leave me a review on Amazon. I appreciate your honest feedback, and it really helps me to continue producing high quality books.

www.ingramcontent.com/pod-product-compliance
Lightning Source LLC
Chambersburg PA
CBHW061324050726
47595CB00005B/1801